CITY IN TIME | New York

CITY IN TIME | New York

WILLIAM HAYES

ORIGINAL PHOTOGRAPHY BY GILBERT KING

STERLING

New York / London
www.sterlingpublishing.com

STERLING and the distinctive Sterling logo are registered trademarks of Sterling Publishing Co., Inc.

Library of Congress Cataloging-in-Publication Data
Hayes, William.
  City in time : New York / William Hayes.
      p. cm.
  Includes index.
  ISBN 978-1-4027-3851-7
1. New York (N.Y.)--History. 2. New York (N.Y.)--Geography. 3. New York (N.Y.)--Pictorial works.
4. Historic buildings--New York (State)--New York. 5. New York (N.Y.)--Buildings, structures, etc. I. Title.

F128.3.H39 2007
974.7'1--dc22

                                                    2006102597

10 9 8 7 6 5 4 3 2

Published by Sterling Publishing Co., Inc.
387 Park Avenue South, New York, NY 10016

© 2007 by Sterling Publishing Co., Inc.
Design by 3+Co.
Cover photo credits: jacket front, Gilbert King; book front, Library of Congress; book / jacket back (top),
Collection of the New York Historical Society negative number 50593; book / jacket back (bottom), Gilbert King

Distributed in Canada by Sterling Publishing
c/o Canadian Manda Group, 165 Dufferin Street
Toronto, Ontario, Canada M6K 3H6

Distributed in the United Kingdom by GMC Distribution Services
Castle Place, 166 High Street, Lewes, East Sussex, England BN7 1XU
Distributed in Australia by Capricorn Link (Australia) Pty. Ltd.
P.O. Box 704, Windsor, NSW 2756, Australia

Sterling ISBN 978-1-4027-3851-7

For information about custom editions, special sales, premium and
corporate purchases, please contact Sterling Special Sales
Department at 800-805-5489 or specialsales@sterlingpublishing.com.

Preface

We hope that this volume of the City in Time series will compel you first to wonder about, then appreciate, and ultimately better understand the development and achievements of the world's great urban centers. The series offers not only interesting time-lapsed juxtapositions, but also meaningful and contrasting images that shed light on the unique resources, circumstances, and creative forces that have propelled these cities to greatness. In a world where renovation and development are so often casually destructive, visual history can be a reservoir of wisdom from which we can inspire and refresh ourselves. We invite you to reflect upon the accomplishments of those who came before us and revel in these impressive monuments to human ambition.

Introduction

New York City—Centuries in the Making

When people think about discovery in the New World, they think of Christopher Columbus. In fact, it was another Italian, Giovanni da Verrazzano, who is believed to have been the first European to sail into New York in 1524. At the time of its European discovery, the region was inhabited by the Lenape tribe of Native Americans, sometimes referred to as the "Manahatta Indians" for which Manhattan was supposedly named. By 1613, the Dutch had established "New Amsterdam," and in 1626, Peter Minuit purchased the island from the Lenapes for "60 guilders" or about $24 worth of goods.

In 1674, the city was ceded to the British, who held it until the last ships evacuated after the American Revolution in 1783. New York's post–Revolutionary War population more than doubled in less than ten years, a growth spurt that enabled it to surpass Philadelphia and Boston in terms of economic vitality. Completion of the Erie Canal on October 26, 1825, opened the country west of the Appalachian Mountains to settlers and offered a less expensive and safer method of bringing goods to a market.

The results of the canal were obvious immediately. New York City became synonymous with a promised land that offered plenty of opportunity, a place that drew immigrants from Germany and Italy, Russia and Ireland, Hungary, and other European countries. Toward the end of the 19th century, they would sail into the Upper Bay and see the Statue of Liberty standing majestically—her torch raised as a beacon for all to see. Upon their arrival, immigrants would disperse into strange new neighborhoods that were often divided by ethnicity. Many would settle in ghettos and fight disease and poverty not unlike the hardships they'd left behind. But many also participated in the ever-growing economy and laid the foundation for future generations of New Yorkers and Americans to prosper.

New York began to soar into the sky by the turn of the 20th century. In lower Manhattan, buildings began to crowd the skyline, eventually dwarfing the impressive vision of the Statue of Liberty—a symbol of the economic might New York now wielded. "It is not an architectural vision," architecture critic Montgomery Schuyler declared, "but it does, most tremendously, look like business."

Steel-frame construction and elevators were perfected, enabling New York to continue building higher and higher. Bridges to Brooklyn and Queens also allowed the city to expand outward. By the 1930s, with the construction of the Chrysler Building and the Empire State Building, New York City had become one of those rare places—perhaps the only place in the world—where man seemed to have completely shaped the environment.

Change, though, was inevitable. The city grew taller, for sure, but before long, the new was beginning to devour the old. Some of the city's greatest structures were ultimately demolished to make room for newer, more cost-effective architecture. The new is embraced—stunning visions of the future for the world to emulate—yet the past is preserved and treasured, often in the same vista. Such is the charm and the wonder of New York City.

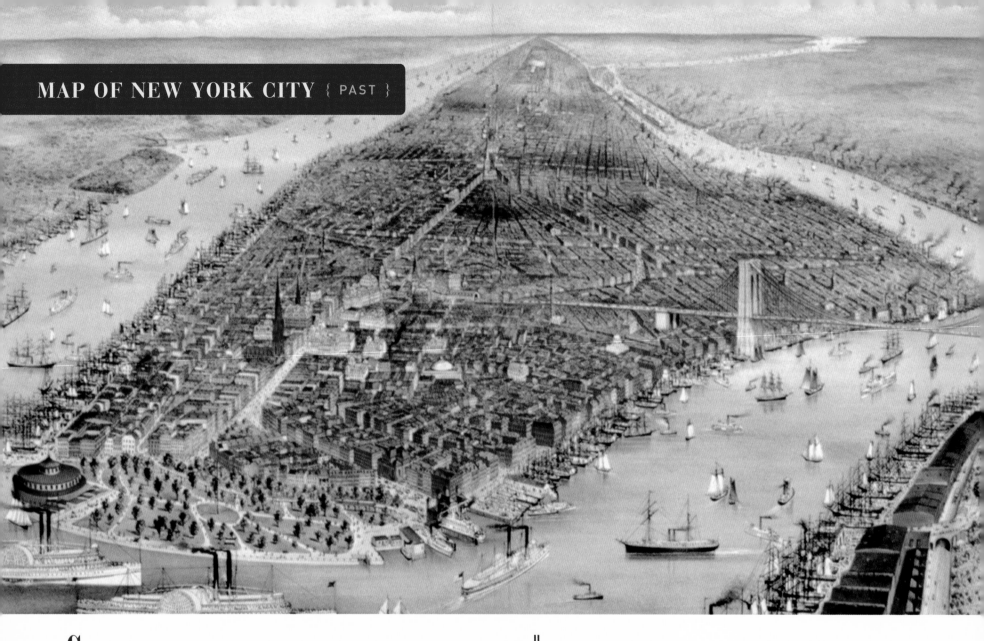

Created in 1884 by the famous 19th-century lithographic firm, Currier & Ives, this bird's-eye view of Manhattan, overlooking the south end of the island, portrays New York as the busy, thriving harbor city it once was. Ships and boats filled the waterways, and the Brooklyn Bridge, newly built, stretches across the East River—bringing the outer borough into reach of Manhattan in just the time it took to cross it.

Taken from miles above the earth, this satellite image of New York City provides a vivid perspective of the city's vast growth and expansion into the 21st century. No longer is the Brooklyn Bridge the only expanse that reaches into the outer boroughs, as the Manhattan, the Williamsburg, the Queensborough, and the Triborough bridges are clearly visible. So too is Ground Zero, the brown patch of land in lower Manhattan to the west.

Collection of the New York Historical Society negative number 50593

A gift from France, the Statue of Liberty was dedicated in 1886 and eventually became one of the most recognizable icons in the United States. Lady Liberty continues to represent to the world the escape from oppression that inspired millions to sail for America from countries like Germany, Ireland, and Italy. Located on Liberty Island (known as Bedloe's Island until 1956), Lady Liberty stands 305 feet high, including the pedestal and foundation, and weighs 204 tons.

LORE & LEGEND

Liberty Island is actually within the borders of New Jersey but has been part of New York since a 1664 charter.

LORE & LEGEND

Emma Lazarus's "The New Colossus" was engraved on a bronze plaque in 1903 and is located on a wall of the museum—not on the base of the statue, as many believe.

Liberty Island was closed on September 11, 2001, and wasn't reopened again until December of that year. The interior of the statue was also closed because of security concerns, but a glass ceiling in the museum's pedestal permits visitors to view the statue's inner structure. A new torch replaced the original, which was deemed beyond repair, but the 1886 torch is located in the museum for viewing.

On January 1, 1892, Ellis Island, at the mouth of the Hudson River in New York Harbor, became the main port of entry for immigrants seeking a better life in the United States. Designed by architects Edward Lippincott Tilton and William Boring, Ellis Island was the processing point for more than twelve million immigrants, who were hopeful of making their dreams a reality. However, approximately two percent of immigrants were denied admission to the United States and sent back to their homelands for reasons such as disease, insanity, or criminal history. Ellis Island earned the nickname "The Island of Hope, the Island of Tears."

ELLIS ISLAND { PRESENT }

Ellis Island processed 70 percent of all immigrants coming into the United States at the turn of the 20th century until "Quota Laws" in 1924 restricted the number allowed into the country. During World War II, Ellis Island was used mostly as a detention facility, where Japanese were interned, along with German-Americans falsely accused of being Nazis. The facility was eventually closed in 1954 and fell into disrepair until it was restored in 1990. Today, Ellis Island houses a museum under the management of the National Park Service and is dedicated to the history of immigration to America.

Castle Clinton, or Fort Clinton, was a circular sandstone fort in Battery Park—the southernmost tip of Manhattan—built in 1812 to defend New York from invading English forces. The fort was originally constructed on an island known as "West Battery," but when a landfill expanded Battery Park, the fort was relocated onto the island of Manhattan. Until 1855, Castle Garden, as it was renamed, became the Emigrant Landing Depot for immigration processing, until the Ellis Island facility was completed in 1892.

Battery Park City—named for Battery Park, which lines the water—is now the site of the World Financial Center, as well as residential housing and retail buildings. Castle Clinton, renovated in the 1970s, is administered by the National Park Service today and contains a museum. The fort is nestled in the trees to the left in this photo, as skyscrapers around the Wall Street area dominate the skyline. Battery Park City has experienced a residential rebirth, as many young Wall Street and World Financial Center employees working long hours created a demand for nearby housing.

One of New York's earliest open-air fish markets, the Fulton Fish Market was established in 1822 and was the most well-known wholesale fish market on the East Coast. Located near the Brooklyn Bridge along the East River, it often was the final destination for fishing boats across the Atlantic. For more than 180 years, it was here that fish were unloaded in the early-morning hours and sold to retailers and restaurateurs. The Fulton Fish Market survived major fires in 1835, 1945, 1918, and again in 1995.

In November 2005, the Fulton Fish Market relocated to a multimillion-dollar, modern facility in the Hunts Point section of the Bronx, putting an end to more than 180 years of the fish trade in Manhattan and glorious sunrises over the Brooklyn Bridge for the 600 workers who arrived at the market in the early hours. The stalls still remain, but the signs marking each company, much they way they did more than 100 years ago, are gone. The cobblestone streets and buildings around the near by South Street Seaport are a landmarked district.

The first location for the New York Stock and Exchange Board (renamed the NYSE in 1863) was a room at 40 Wall Street in 1817 that was rented for $200 a month. In September 1920, a horse-drawn wagon stopped across from the J.P. Morgan & Co. bank headquarters with a large amount of dynamite and cast-iron slugs aboard. The bomb was detonated, killing 33 people and injuring more than 400 in the blast. Evidence of the bombing can still be seen on the facades of nearby buildings, including the New York Stock Exchange.

The New York Stock Exchange is the largest stock exchange in the United States, with a global capitalization of more than $21 trillion. There are 1,366 seats on the exchange, a number that has not changed since 1953, and the most expensive seat on the exchange was sold in 1929 for $625,000 (more than $6 million in today's dollars). Tourists continue to flock to Wall Street to get photographs of themselves in front of this building, the greatest symbol of capitalism in the world.

Founded in 1766 by converted Methodists from Ireland, the John Street Church was taken over by the British Army in 1776, though pastor Samuel Spraggs was permitted to continue services for American parishioners. The original chapel was torn down in 1817 to make room for a larger structure, which opened four years later. The chapel seen here in this photograph was built in 1841, and the Georgian-inspired design features a brownstone facade. John Street Church has been declared a New York City landmark building.

JOHN STREET CHURCH { PRESENT }

The oldest Methodist congregation in the United States, John Street Church is now a United Methodist Church, but the interior and furnishings remain much as they were in 1841. Below the church, the Wesley Chapel Museum has many artifacts from the 18th and 19th centuries on display, including church record books, class-meeting circular benches, and an altar rail from 1785. Visitors to the museum can also participate in an hour-long guided tour to learn more about the early-American religious movement.

Collection of the New York Historical Society negative number 59174

The heart of New York's financial district is seen here at Broad Street—a small street that stretches from South to Wall Streets. Broad Street was named for the Broad Canal, an inlet from the East River, which was filled in 1676. This photograph from 1912 shows the famous "Curb Brokers" who dealt in a daily, animated open-air market for the sale and trade of stocks not listed on the Exchanges. The columned building in the rear is Federal Hall, where George Washington was inaugurated in 1789 as the first President of the United States.

Some of the buildings are gone, but the corner of Wall Street and Broad still represents the heart of the world's financial markets, and its landmark buildings remain. The New York Stock Exchange is still located at 18 Broad Street, and the area is home to many of the city's major financial institutions. Curb brokers have been replaced by Internet day traders, but the financial district still buzzes with activity on weekdays, while becoming eerily quiet on weekends.

New York's Skyscrapers—A Visual History of the World's Tallest Buildings

There were several factors responsible for the growth of high-rise buildings in New York City at the turn of the 20th century. Two engineering developments—William Le Baron Jenney's use of steel-frame construction and David Lindquist's gearless-traction elevator—inspired building designers to aim for the skies in Manhattan.

With dwindling land plots becoming more expensive, corporations had no choice but to expand upward rather than outward in New York. The stable bedrock below the island of Manhattan's surface provided the perfect base for "skyscrapers," a term coined by sailors who used it to describe a ship's tallest mast and compare them to the city's tallest buildings.

When Trinity Church was completed in 1846 in lower Manhattan, its soaring neo-Gothic spire dominated the skyline. Since then, nearly a dozen buildings in New York have been, at one time, the tallest building in the world.

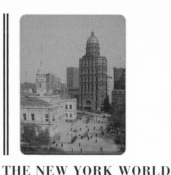

THE NEW YORK WORLD BUILDING *(1890)*
The New York World Building was located on "Newspaper Row" opposite City Hall for Joseph Pulitzer's *New York World*. At 309 feet, the World Building was the tallest in the world.

MANHATTAN LIFE INSURANCE COMPANY BUILDING *(1894)*
At 348 feet, it was the world's tallest building for five years.

WOOLWORTH BUILDING *(1913)*
This beautiful Gothic-style building stands 792 feet and was illuminated in an opening ceremony when President Woodrow Wilson pressed a button in the White House, lighting both the interior and exterior.

THE MANHATTAN COMPANY *(1930)*
Part of the 1929 race for the world's tallest tower, the Manhattan Company building reached 927 feet but did not hold the title for long.

ST. PAUL BUILDING *(1898)*

At 315 feet, it was designed by George B. Post and named after St. Paul's Chapel, which is located across the street on Broadway.

PARK ROW BUILDING *(1899)*

The Park Row Building, at 391 feet above the sidewalk, was the world's tallest. It still stands today.

SINGER BUILDING *(1908)*

At 612 feet, the home to the sewing machine company became the tallest in the world by a long shot but only held the title for a year.

THE CHRYSLER BUILDING *(1931)*

Architect William Van Alen, caught up in the race for the tallest building, unveiled a secret 185-foot spire at the end of construction to bring the Chrysler Building to a height of 1,046 feet, topping the Manhattan Company building.

THE EMPIRE STATE BUILDING *(1932)*

At 1,250 feet, this famous building was designed and erected in just twenty months, and held the title of world's tallest for thirty nine years.

THE WORLD TRADE CENTER *(1971)*

Construction began in 1966 and when finished five years later, both towers topped the Empire State Building by 100 feet. The towers fell on September 11, 2001.

Completed in 1846, the first Trinity Church in lower Manhattan dominated the island's skyline with its impressive Neo-Gothic spire. The parish was granted by King William III, who specified an annual rent of one peppercorn, payable to the English crown. Located on the corner of Broadway and Wall Street, approaching ships from miles out in the Atlantic used the church as a beacon. It seems entirely appropriate that Alexander Hamilton, the first U.S. Secretary of the Treasury, is buried in the Trinity Churchyard on Wall Street.

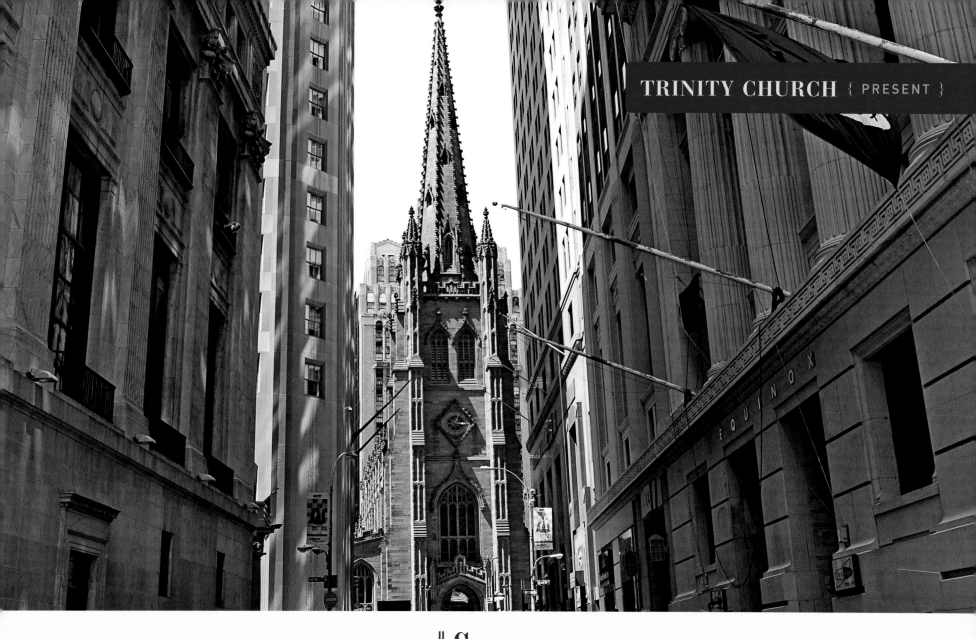

Skyscrapers have been built all around Trinity Church, and unlike the days of 19th-century ship captains, it takes some effort to see the spire today. The church is run by the Episcopal Diocese of New York and is known for its music program, including the Trinity Choir. The Trinity Churchyard Cemetery is the last and only active cemetery in Manhattan. A classic example of Gothic Revival architecture, Trinity Church has been designated a National Historic Landmark.

New York City Hall was designed by John McComb Jr. and Joseph François Mangin, with construction beginning in 1803 and lasting for nine years. The building's facade is made of granite and marble in the front and sandstone to the rear, and Harvard University later modeled its own buildings on City Hall's distinctive cupola. The three-story building features the Governor's Room, which has served as a museum and reception room that celebrates the civic history of New York and America. In 1861, the room hosted President-elect Abraham Lincoln and also served as the backdrop for his coffin four years later when he lay in state.

City Hall houses both the New York City Council and the mayor's office. Today, fences surround the City Hall building and access is restricted. But any number of protesters, calling attention to their causes, can be found just outside the gates of City Hall, a designated New York City landmark. The official setting for mayoral press conferences is located in the building's "Blue Room," and the nearby Manhattan Municipal Building houses the mayor's staff and municipal agencies.

PARK ROW { PAST }

Once known as "Newspaper Row," Park Row earned its former nickname when New York newspapers of the day wanted their offices to be close to all the action at City Hall. At one time, there were fifteen daily newspapers located there, including the *New York Times*, which relocated uptown in 1905, and the now-defunct *New York World* and *New York Tribune* newspapers. Just south of City Hall, the spire from St. Paul's Chapel can be seen in the distance in this photograph from 1865.

Today, the Park Row area is still home to St. Paul's Chapel. St. Paul's was completed in 1766 and, at the time, stood in a field away from the main city of New York to the south. Following the attack on September 11, 2001, St. Paul's Chapel (which miraculously survived without even a broken window, despite its close proximity to the Twin Towers) served as a resting place for recovery workers and as an impromptu memorial where visitors placed flowers, photos, and other mementos to honor the dead.

NEW·YORK·LIFE·
BUILDING
·346·BROADWAY·

Though it was never a competitor in the "tallest building in New York" race, the twelve-story New York Life Building at 346 Broadway was one of the most impressive of the 19th-century skyscrapers that jutted into the downtown Manhattan skyline. Designed by the firm of McKim, Mead & White, the palazzo-style building was completed in 1898 and was an immediate testament to the permanence and stability that the New York Life Insurance wanted to convey.

Today, the building at 346 Broadway—with its terra-cotta ceiling at the entrance, its marble wainscoting, beautiful metalwork, and marbled Presidential Suite (the most decorative interior room in the building)—has been designated a landmark by the Landmarks Preservation Commission. Parts of the interior have fallen into disrepair, and the building is now owned by the city and used for offices and criminal court procedures. But the 250,000-square foot building seems destined for apartment conversion, as has been the fate of many of these classic structures in downtown New York.

At the turn of the 20th century, Doyers Street in Chinatown was a dangerous place to be after dark—a crooked street where violence, mayhem, and gang warfare earned it the nickname of "the Bloody Angle." Secret Chinese societies called "Tongs" were engaged in drug trade, prostitution, and other illegal activities, and New York's "Tong Wars" were particularly violent in Chinatown. Gang members would bide their time and ambush rivals around the bend. In 1909, it's believed that some fifty Chinese men were murdered in the vicinity of the Bloody Angle.

Today, Chinatown is among the safer communities in New York. Bustling twenty-four hours a day, many restaurants are open late and marketplaces open very early. Chinatown still is home to an underground economy and is where large numbers of immigrants are able to immediately begin work upon their arrival in the United States. Working in the garment industry or in restaurants, these immigrants earn low wages and work long hours. Doyers Street is one of the narrow Chinatown streets that seems to hearken back to an earlier era in New York.

Pell Street, which connects the Bowery and Doyers Street, was a bustling corner in Chinatown where little tea salons, shops, and tenements sprang up in the late 1800s to accommodate the influx of Chinese immigrants into lower Manhattan. The Tong Wars in Chinatown led to the formation of associations that aided in providing business loans, as well as protection and mediation in disputes between Tong groups. But these Tongs often drifted into criminal activities, such as gambling, extortion, human smuggling, and prostitution, which flourished in lower Manhattan.

Pell Street today does not look much different than it did more than 100 years ago. The names of the restaurants, barbershops, and tea salons may have changed, but the corner of Pell and Doyers is still alive with business activity. The Tongs that had infiltrated everyday life in Chinatown disappeared in the late 1980s, and crime in Chinatown—as in all of New York City—has decreased dramatically.

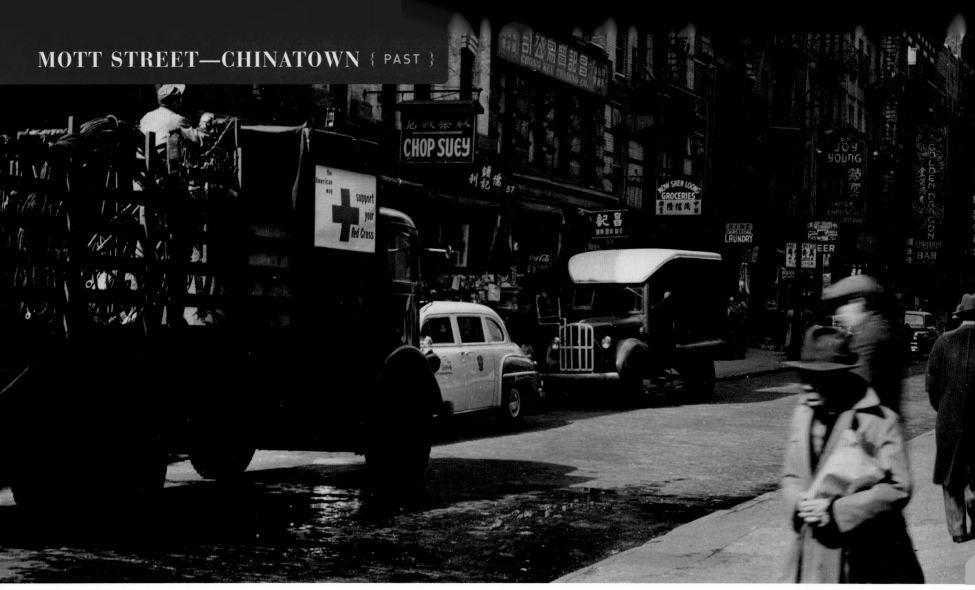

Collection of the New York Historical Society

Mott Street has been the "Main Street" of New York City's Chinatown section since the late 1800s, when Chinese immigrants began to settle around Chinese merchant Wo Kee's general store in 1872. By 1900, there were more than 7,000 Chinese residents in Chinatown, and the street's fish and vegetable markets and restaurants made Mott Street one of the busiest streets in the city. The narrow thoroughfare through Chinatown was laid out in the late 1700s and had bends in it that meandered around New York's Collect Pond, since drained.

Today, New York's Chinatown has grown into the largest in the United States, and Mott Street continues to be the center of it. Souvenir shops, tea houses, and restaurants attract both tourists and locals, but aside from the names of the businesses, very little has changed over the years. Chinatown has continued to expand north of Canal Street, taking over buildings and shops that were predominantly part of Little Italy not long ago.

A t the turn of the 20th century, Hester Street was synonymous with "the ghetto" or the "Tenth Ward," or, as Jacob Riis called it, "Jew Town." The Chazzer Market teemed with pushcarts where Jewish peddlers (schleppers) sold a variety of goods—from fruit to bandannas, at bargain prices. Historically a center for Ashkenazi (descending primarily from Eastern Europe) Jewish immigrant culture, Hester Street also attracted other immigrant groups seeking bargains, creating a brash, multinational bazaar that only could exist in New York at the time.

Today, Hester Street has very little evidence of the marketplace that existed 100 years ago. The pushcarts are gone and so are most of the Yiddish signs in storefronts. But the area still boasts a multicultural environment. Chinese and Latino immigrants have been settling on the Lower East Side for decades now, but gentrification in the area has driven real estate prices up and many immigrants out.

At the turn of the 20th century, Little Italy extended as far uptown as Bleeker Street and as far downtown as Bayard Street. It also went as far east as the Bowery and as far west as Lafayette Street. At the center of it all was Mulberry Street, which, in many respects, became the heart of Italian-American culture. Here, during Fiesta, pushcarts and stands selling Italian cheeses and other goods lined up on both sides of Mulberry Street, where the street market thrived.

LORE & LEGEND

The Mafia's power in the mid-20th century had its American roots in New York's Little Italy, after "Black Hand" gangsters would extort Italian-owned (and other) businesses around the city. Several prominent factions—

such as the Colombo, Bonanno, and Gambino families—dominated New York, and their frequent turf wars were often documented in the headlines of the city's tabloid newspapers.

The boundaries of Little Italy may have shrunk over the years, but Mulberry Street remains the heart of New York's Italian culture, which is evident each year during the Feast of San Gennaro. What used to be a one-day religious ceremony has now become an eleven-day street fair in mid-September, when Mulberry Street is blocked off to motor traffic, food is eaten, and typical street games, such as ring toss and darts, are played late into the evening.

Italian immigrants came to New York in great numbers in the late 1800s when poverty and unemployment were rampant in Italy. By 1920, it was estimated that nearly 400,000 Italians were living in New York—and the majority of them settled in the area known as Little Italy in lower Manhattan, where they often clustered in sections based on the regions from which they emigrated. First Avenue just above Houston Street was a busy market, where Italian-Americans could purchase foods and vegetables and bring Italian cuisine across the Atlantic.

As Italian-Americans began to flee the city for the suburbs in droves during the 1950s, Little Italy began to shrink. The area above Houston Street on First Avenue is now known as NoLita (**NO**rth of **LI**ttle **ITA**ly), and there are few reminders of the Avenue's past and its importance to Italian immigrants. NoLita is considered a trendy residential area now, with boutique shops and restaurants cropping up on a regular basis. But Little Italy is still a popular destination for tourists because of the many fine and casual Italian restaurants and cafes, new and old.

Collection of the New York Historical Society

I n 1820, the Collect Pond was drained for health reasons, and the value of the swampy, insect-ridden land attracted little interest, save from the poor immigrants who were flooding into the city. The area—known as the "Five Points"—became one of the most notorious slums the world had ever seen, with horrendous living conditions. In the late 1880s, slum clearance efforts managed to raze Five Points. A correctional facility, the infamous Tombs Prison, stood just to the north of the corner of Centre Street and Reade Street, pictured here in 1908.

Construction began in 1909 on the Manhattan Municipal Building as part of the City Beautiful Movement. Beneath the Roman-influenced building, the architectural firm of McKim, Mead & White incorporated New York's first subway station—magnificently tiled and ornate—just below street level. One of the largest governmental buildings in the world, the 40-story Municipal Building is where nearly 30,000 New Yorkers are married each year, and the building accommodates more than 2,000 city employees, in nearly one million square feet of floor space.

The New York City Subway

By the mid-1800s, New York City—which had already been building upward to accommodate the dwindling amount of real estate in Manhattan—was making plans that would enable New Yorkers to expand below ground as well. In 1863, London had an underground subway system running, and by 1874, New York had begun construction of an underwater tunnel that would connect Manhattan with New Jersey. But nothing was as ambitious as the New York subway system that would ultimately link the boroughs of the city with an immense underground railroad powered by electricity. Just as remarkable as the plan itself was the execution. A private firm, the Interborough Rapid Transit Company, would need just four years to complete more than twenty miles of subway line, and on October 27, 1904, the city's first passengers were traveling underground.

Mayor George B. McClellan headed the festivities, taking control of the first train and rocketing it up from City Hall to 103rd Street at nearly fifty miles per hour. Later that evening, the subway was opened to the general public, who paid five cents for a ride. By the weekend, the subway had accommodated more than a million people who waited in lines running up the stairs and, often times, around the block. Wealthy New Yorkers rode the trains out of curiosity, but the subway transformed the lives of working New Yorkers, who were soon able to live outside the crowded streets of Manhattan and still commute to the city for work. Just a few years later, the subway was transporting nearly a million riders a day.

Over the following decade, more than 600 miles of railroad track were added to the system, making it possible to travel from Brooklyn to the Bronx by way of Manhattan for just a nickel. But more importantly, the subway enabled immigrants the opportunity to escape the ghettos of the Lower East Side and take root in Brooklyn, Queens, and the Bronx, while still having the ability to work in Manhattan. New, privately owned systems, such as the Brooklyn Rapid Transit Company, sprang up, allowing further expansion of subway lines, until the New York City Transit Authority was created in 1953. The Metropolitan Transit Authority assumed control of public transportation in New York in 1968. But today, the system is operated by the New York City Transit Authority.

FACTS AND FIGURES

DAILY RIDERS	4,800,000	TOKEN BOOTHS	734
SYSTEM LENGTH	842 MILES	LONGEST RIDE	31 MILES (THE A TRAIN FROM 207TH STREET IN MANHATTAN TO FAR ROCKAWAY IN QUEENS)
TOTAL STATIONS	468		
TURNSTILES	31,180	BUSIEST STATION	TIMES SQUARE
ESCALATORS	161		

MULBERRY BEND { PAST }

When Jacob Riis went to work for the *South Brooklyn News* in 1874, he set up an office in Mulberry Bend, in the heart of a tenement neighborhood, and each day he set out to witness the harsh living conditions of slum life in 19th-century New York. He eventually learned to take photographs, and in 1890, he published his book, *How the Other Half Lives*, which exposed the squalor and societal problems around Mulberry Bend. This photograph (not by Riis) shows a clam seller peddling his seafood in 1900.

When the Five Points area was razed, a park was erected, alternately named Mulberry Bend Park, Five Points Park, and Paradise Park until it received its present name, Columbus Park, in 1911. Riis himself was happy to see the slums torn down and the trees, grass, and flowers take its place. Today—after an infusion of Italian, German, and Irish immigrants populated the area—Mulberry Bend is a thriving part of Chinatown. The east side of Mulberry Street, seen here, is lined with funeral homes that serve the Chinatown district.

The Brooklyn Bridge took thirteen years to build, cost more than $15 million, and saw nearly thirty people die during its construction. When it was finally opened on May 24, 1883, it was the longest suspension bridge in the world. Its two towers—built from granite, limestone, and cement— were also the tallest structures in the Western Hemisphere for many years. When designer John Augustus Roebling died from tetanus nine years into construction, his son, Washington, took the reins. When he was stricken by caisson disease, his wife and aide, Emily Warren Roebling, acted as his liaison during construction and was one of the first people to cross the bridge upon its completion.

The Brooklyn Bridge remains one of the oldest and most prominent cultural landmarks in New York City, as people have long marveled at its construction as a symbol of the optimism that prevailed at the time it was built. The most photographed bridge in New York, and perhaps the world, the Brooklyn Bridge has appeared in key scenes of numerous movies over the years. The Brooklyn Bridge Park Conservancy organizes events year-round, including music, dance, and outdoor film screenings.

Spanning nearly 6,000 feet over the East River and connecting Brooklyn with Manhattan, the Brooklyn Bridge is 85 feet wide and allows 135 feet of clearance at mid-span. John Augustus Roebling designed the bridge to be six times stronger than required—part of the reason why the bridge has proven to be so durable, while others just as old have crumbled or decayed more rapidly. Less than a week after the bridge opened in 1883, a rumor quickly spread that the bridge was about to collapse. A stampede ensued, and twelve people were crushed to death.

O ver the years, the Brooklyn Bridge has carried trolleys, horses, and streetcars, and elevated trains even ran on two center lanes until 1944. Today, there are six lanes for motor vehicles to cross from Brooklyn into Manhattan and back, with no tolls. But there's no better way to cross the Brooklyn Bridge than by foot or bicycle, which thousands of people do each day—either to commute, for exercise, or simply to see the sights.

The intersection at Broadway and Canal Street was a congested one, even in 1875 when this photograph was taken. Horse-drawn carriages drew many to this downtown area—popular with art lovers, as successful galleries sprang up with regularity. But the majority of people in lower Manhattan were still recent immigrants, who provided goods and services in the many shops that lined the thoroughfare.

Today, the intersection at Broadway and Canal Street is in the area known as SoHo (**SO**uth of **HO**uston Street), where artists flocked in the 1960s because of the abundance of inexpensive loft spaces that could be found. Real estate prices have forced many artists to move to areas such as Williamsburg and Greenpoint in Brooklyn, and Long Island City in Queens, making room for the expensive boutiques, restaurants, and galleries that now populate SoHo. The intersection is still busy with traffic today, albeit a more modern mode.

The Collect Pond, which was a body of water just west of where Chinatown is today, was a source of fresh water for Manhattan residents in the early 1800s. But as the city grew, the pond became polluted—slaughterhouses, factories, and tanneries all contributed to the water's contamination—and diseases such as typhus and cholera threatened residents. The Collect was drained and a canal was constructed the length of Manhattan between the Hudson and East rivers. In 1820, the canal was filled and became Canal Street.

The east side of Canal Street is a busy commercial district known for street vendors, seafood markets, jewelry shops, hardware, and other cheap goods. On the west side, Canal Street intersects with Hudson Street near the entrance of the Holland Tunnel, which links Manhattan and New Jersey and was completed in 1927. The area marks the northern border of TriBeCa (**TRI**angle **BE**low **CA**nal), where many warehouses have been converted to residential lofts, transforming the neighborhood into a trendy, upscale community.

Washington Square Park has been the center of cultural life in New York's Greenwich Village since the mid-1800s, and is a landmark that calls to mind the non-conformity of both the artistic and political climates of the times. The park is best known for its Memorial Arch, erected in 1889 at the northern entrance to the park at Fifth Avenue to celebrate the centennial of George Washington's inauguration as president of the United States. Another of the park's characteristics is a grand fountain, which was completed in 1852.

LET US RAISE A STANDARD TO WHICH THE WISE AND THE HONEST CAN REPAIR THE EVENT IS IN THE HAND OF GOD WASHINGTON

After World War I, Washington Square Park was a gathering place for many writers and artists such as Eugene O'Neill, Willa Cather, and Sinclair Lewis. Aside from the arch and the fountain, a statue commemorating Italian soldier Giuseppe Garibaldi still stands, but a recent redesign plan is threatening to relocate the fountain. A short fence surrounding the park has also been proposed, but lawsuits and appeals have delayed the city's plans. The square is a popular spot for students of New York University, whose buildings surround Washington Square Park.

Uneeda Biscuit
THE NATIONAL SODA CRACKER
Sold only in Packages
5¢
NATIONAL BISCUIT COMPANY

The O.J.Gude Co.,N.Y.
NEW YORK HIPPODROME
The GREATEST SHOW IN THE WORLD
TWICE DAILY

AFTER MEALS — DRINK
Bénédictine
THE BEST CORDIAL

RINGLING B
WORLD'S GREATE

Union Square—situated at the intersection, or union, of two of New York's major thoroughfares, Bloomingdale Road (now Broadway) and Bowery Road (now Fourth Avenue)—was opened to the public in 1839. Its impressive equestrian statue of George Washington was created by Henry Kirke Brown and unveiled in 1856. In April 1861, it was the gathering point for what was believed to be the largest public gathering in North America at the time—a patriotic rally held soon after the fall of Fort Sumter.

Today, the statue of George Washington has been relocated from the southeast corner of the park to the center of the south side of the square. Union Square has continued to serve as a choice location for public meetings, labor protests, and political rallies over the years. In the days following September 11, 2001, Union Square became the central gathering point for candlelight vigils and photograph memorials honoring the victims of the terrorist attacks. Below the park is the Union Square Subway station, which is the eighth-busiest station in New York.

HEINZ

57 GOOD THINGS FOR THE TABLE

PEACH BUTTER

TOMATO SOUP

INDIA RELISH

TOMATO KETCHUP

SWEET PICKLE

The O. J. Gude Co. N.Y.

CHIROPODIST.
ISHAM'S

THE NEW DENTISTRY.

OFFICES TO RENT
IN THESE BUILDINGS
APPLY AT
Room 6 or Room 8
949 Broadway | 111 Broad

MANICURING

PAINLESS METHODS.

SCHOOL OF SCIENCE,
ASTROLOGY, PALMISTRY

Collection of the New York Historical Society negative number 69521

Before architect Daniel Burnham designed the Fuller Building (Flatiron Building), which was completed in 1902, the triangular intersection at 23rd Street between Broadway and Fifth Avenue was the site of the old Cumberland Hotel and home to one of the first electric signs, which dominated the north side of the building. H. J. Heinz saw to it that a 40-foot-long electrified green pickle flashed on and off, and a few of his more popular "57 varieties" such as Indian relish, tomato chutney, and malt vinegar graced the side of the building at different times.

"Have a nice day." citibank NO TURNS

"Thank You" Get points for banking.

citibank

I n 1902, the Flatiron Building was one of the tallest buildings in New York. Today, the 22-story building still stands, but it no longer dominates the skyline. The area has become known as the "Flatiron District" and is home to many photographic studios, restaurants, commercial offices, and residential loft spaces. The Flatiron Building recently underwent a restoration project that involved a cleaning of the facade to reveal tan terra-cotta and brick hidden under decades of grime.

Completed in 1902, the Flatiron Building (known at the time as the Fuller Building) was designed by famed Chicago architect Daniel Burnham with John Wellborn Root. The Beaux Arts–style building, with its Greek columns and terra-cotta facade, was designed to fit in the triangular intersection at Broadway and Fifth Avenue between 22nd and 23rd Streets, and was nicknamed "the Flatiron" because clothing irons of the day were similarly shaped.

The Flatiron Building remains one of the most photographed buildings in New York, in part because of its unique design and in part because of its appearance in films. The Flatiron Building has appeared in *Godzilla*, where it was destroyed by the military, and in *Armageddon*, *Spider-Man* and its sequel (office of the *Daily Bugle*), and *The Usual Suspects*. At twenty-two stories high, it's a National Historic Landmark and is the reason the area is now known as the Flatiron District. Recently renovated, the Flatiron remains as photogenic as ever.

Collection of the New York Historical Society

With Broadway to the east and Madison Avenue to the west, Madison Square, opened to the public in 1847, sits just north of 23rd Street, adjacent to the Flatiron Building. A statue in honor of Secretary of State William H. Seward—who served under Lincoln and Andrew Johnson—sits in the south end of the park, looking out onto 23rd Street. To the east of the park, the Metropolitan Life Insurance Company Tower at 1 Madison Avenue was, in 1909, the tallest building in the world until the Woolworth Building in downtown Manhattan was completed.

LORE & LEGEND

From 1876 to 1882, the arm and the torch from the Statue of Liberty were displayed in the park to raise money for the construction of the statue's base at Liberty Island in Upper New York Bay.

LORE & LEGEND

Legend has it that the phrase "23 skidoo" comes from this very intersection, where men would hang around waiting for the gusts of wind to blow women's dresses up. Police would give the men the "23 skidoo" and shoo them away.

The square was best known for the original Madison Square Garden, which was located at 26th Street and Madison Avenue until it moved to 50th Street and Eighth Avenue in 1925. Today, the square is a newly renovated park—an oasis of green in the busy Flatiron District. An extremely popular outdoor restaurant, Shake Shack, occupies the southwest corner of the square, and Seward's statue continues to look out over 23rd Street. A newly refurbished playground sits in the northeast corner of the square.

Built in 1909, the Metropolitan Life Insurance Company Tower was the world's tallest building until the Woolworth Building surpassed it in 1913. Located directly across the street from Madison Square Park on the southern side of Madison Avenue, the tower was designed by Napoleon LeBrun & Sons, with fifty-two floors and standing 700 feet high. The tower was inspired by the St. Mark's Campanile in Venice, Italy, a free-standing bell tower built in the 8th century as a watchtower.

METROPOLITAN LIFE INSURANCE COMPANY TOWER { PRESENT }

Metropolitan Life maintained its headquarters in the building until 2005, when SL Green Realty Trust purchased the tower with the intent of converting some of the office space into apartments. The tower's exterior was restored in 2002 to include a multicolored night lighting system to signify holidays or events. There are four clocks—one on each side of the tower—and each minute hand weighs half a ton. Originally sheathed in marble, a renovation in 1964 used limestone to cover the tower.

Conceived by Mayor John F. Hylan and built in 1918, New York's Victory Arch was located on Fifth Avenue at 24th Street. The arch was designed by Thomas Hastings and built of wood and other temporary material, including plaster, to honor the city's fallen soldiers during World War I. Fiorello H. LaGuardia, who would become mayor of New York sixteen years later, denounced the project at the time, calling it the "Altar of Extravagance." The temporary arch was razed shortly after the victory parade in 1918.

There are no remains from the 1918 Victory Arch today, but a 51-foot-high obelisk of Quincy granite called the Worth Monument honors Major General William Jenkins Worth (1794–1849), a well-respected military tactician who fought in the Mexican-American War. The monument was placed at this intersection in 1857 and blended with the Victory Arch temporary statues. Today, the Empire State Building commands the view looking north from 23rd Street.

New York—A Rich, Artistic History in Quotes

New York City has been home to some of the greatest artists and writers in the world—whether they were born and raised there or simply heeded the city's siren call. Ponder the following words and phrases inspired by New York:

HENRY JAMES

In crossing Union Square, in front of the monument to Washington, in the very shadow, indeed, projected by the image of the pater patrie—one of them remarked to the other, "It seems a rum-looking place."

—HENRY JAMES

I have never walked down Fifth Avenue alone without thinking of money.

—ANTHONY TROLLOPE

A million people—manners free and superb—open voices—hospitality—the most courageous and friendly young men, City of hurried and sparkling waters! city of spires and masts! City nested in bays! my city!

—WALT WHITMAN

The present in New York is so powerful that the past is lost.

—JOHN JAY CHAPMAN

New York City is inhabited by 4,000,000 mysterious strangers; thus beating Bird Centre by three millions and half a dozen nine's. They came here in various ways and for many reasons—Hendrik Hudson, the art schools, green goods, the stork, the annual dressmakers' convention, the Pennsylvania Railroad, love of money, the stage, cheap excursion rates, brains, personal column ads, heavy walking shoes, ambition, freight trains—all these have had a hand in making up the population.

—O. HENRY

THOMAS WOLFE

It was a cruel city, but it was a lively one, a savage city, yet it had such tenderness; a bitter, harsh and violent catacomb of stone and steel and tunneled rock, slashed savagely with light, and roaring, fighting a constant ceaseless warfare of men and machinery . . . .

—THOMAS WOLFE

So here we are in New-York. To a Frenchman the aspect of the city is bizarre and not very agreeable. One sees neither dome, nor bell tower, nor great edifice, with the result that one has the constant impression of being in a suburb.

—ALEXIS DE TOCQUEVILLE

F. SCOTT FITZGERALD

New York had all the iridescence of the beginning of the world. The returning troops marched up Fifth Avenue and girls were instinctively drawn East and North toward them—this was the greatest nation and there was gala in the air.

—F. SCOTT FITZGERALD

On Broadway it was still bright afternoon and the gassy air was almost motionless under the leaden spokes of sunlight, and sawdust footprints lay about the doorways of butcher shops and fruit stores. And the great, great crowd, the inexhaustible current of millions of every race and kind pouring out, pressing round, of every age, of every genius, possessors of every human secret, antique and future.

—SAUL BELLOW

Over the great bridge, with the sunlight through the girders making a constant flicker upon the moving cars, with the city rising up across the river in white heaps and sugar lumps all built with a wish out of non-olfactory money. The city seen from the Queensboro Bridge is always the city seen for the first time, in its first wild promise of all the mystery and the beauty in the world.

—F. SCOTT FITZGERALD

It can destroy an individual, or it can fulfill him, depending a good deal on luck. No one should come to New York to live unless he is willing to be lucky.

—E.B. WHITE

A New York divorce is in itself a diploma of virtue.

—EDITH WHARTON

And New York is the most beautiful city in the world? It is not far from it. No urban night is like the night there . . . . Squares after squares of flame, set up and cut into the aether. Here is our poetry, for we have pulled down the stars to our will.

—EZRA POUND

HELEN KELLER

Cut off as I am, it is inevitable that I should sometimes feel like a shadow walking in a shadowy world. When this happens I ask to be taken to New York City. Always I return home weary but I have the comforting certainty that mankind is real flesh and I myself am not a dream.

—HELEN KELLER

Once a passenger depot, the building at 26th street and Madison Avenue was converted by P. T. Barnum into "Barnum's Monster Classical and Geological Hippodrome," which was later renamed "Gilmore's Garden" in 1876. But William Henry Vanderbilt officially renamed the building "Madison Square Garden" and opened it to the public in 1879 for the sport of track cycling. Renowned architect Stanford White designed the second Madison Square Garden, which opened at the same site in 1890.

Madison Square Garden was torn down in the early 1920s and a new one was erected on the west side of Manhattan in 1925. In its place, designer Cass Gilbert, also the architect of the Woolworth Building, built the New York Life Insurance Building in 1926. That was completed in 1928, rises forty stories with a pyramid-shaped gilded roof, and has been designated an official New York City Landmark.

Built in slightly more than one year, the Empire State Building was hurried to completion in 1931 so that it would overtake the title of "world's tallest building" from the nearby Chrysler Building, which had held the honor since 1928. Designed by the firm of Shreve, Lamb and Harmon, the 102-story Art Deco skyscraper was named one of the Seven Wonders of the Modern World by the American Society of Civil Engineers. It remained the tallest building in the world until the World Trade Center towers were built in the early 1970s.

LORE & LEGEND

The Empire State Building has been featured in numerous films, but none so famous as the 1933 version of *King Kong*. In it, Kong climbs the building with his beauty in hand, until he is gunned down by fighter planes. To celebrate the film's

50th anniversary, a giant, eight-story inflatable King Kong was suspended atop the building, but high winds tore a large hole along the seam, leaving, as the *New York Times* reported, "the deflated ape looking like a 3,000-pound garbage bag."

Since the terrorist attacks of September 11, 2001, the Empire State Building has regained its status as New York's tallest skyscraper. The lobby is three stories high and the north corridor features illuminated panels, which were added to the building in 1963 and designed by Roy Sparkia and Renee Nemorov, depicting the building as the Eighth Wonder of the World. The observatory on the 86th floor is a popular destination for tourists, who can enjoy the views, on clear days, for miles in all directions.

Named for the *International Herald Tribune*—which was founded in 1887 and headquartered at the intersection of Broadway, Sixth Avenue, and 34th Street—Herald Square was the home of two of the largest retail stores in the world, Gimbel's and Macy's. Macy's opened in 1902, followed by Gimbel's across the street in 1910. Their competition lasted for decades. George M. Cohan's song, "Give My Regards to Broadway," features the line, "Remember me to Herald Square."

LORE & LEGEND

The star in the Macy's logo comes from a tattoo its founder, Rowland Hussey Macy, got as a teenager when he worked on a whaling ship out of Nantucket.

LORE & LEGEND

Longtime Macy's co-owner Isidor Straus was one of the *Titanic*'s most famous casualties when he perished aboard the ship, along with his wife, Ida.

Gimbel's closed in 1987, and the site where Gimbel's stood is now the Manhattan Mall, but the area—just ten blocks south of Times Square—is still a retail haven. Sitting adjacent to the site of the former New York Herald Building is Greeley Square, a small park named for Horace Greeley, editor of the *New York Tribune*, which was one of America's most influential newspapers from 1840–1870. The Macy's Thanksgiving Day Parade, which, since 1945, has begun on the Upper West Side of Manhattan, ends as it passes the Macy's store on 7th Avenue.

Collection of the New York Historical Society negative number 69523

There is an odd notch at the corner of Broadway and 34th Street at Herald Square—the result of a holdout in the late 1890s, when Macy's architects, DeLemos & Cordes, built around the small corner store, whose owner did not, at the time, agree to terms with the department store's offer to relocate it. In 1903, the stubborn owner demolished the building, and replaced it with a five-story structure designed by William H. Hume, which he originally leased to the United Cigar Store Company.

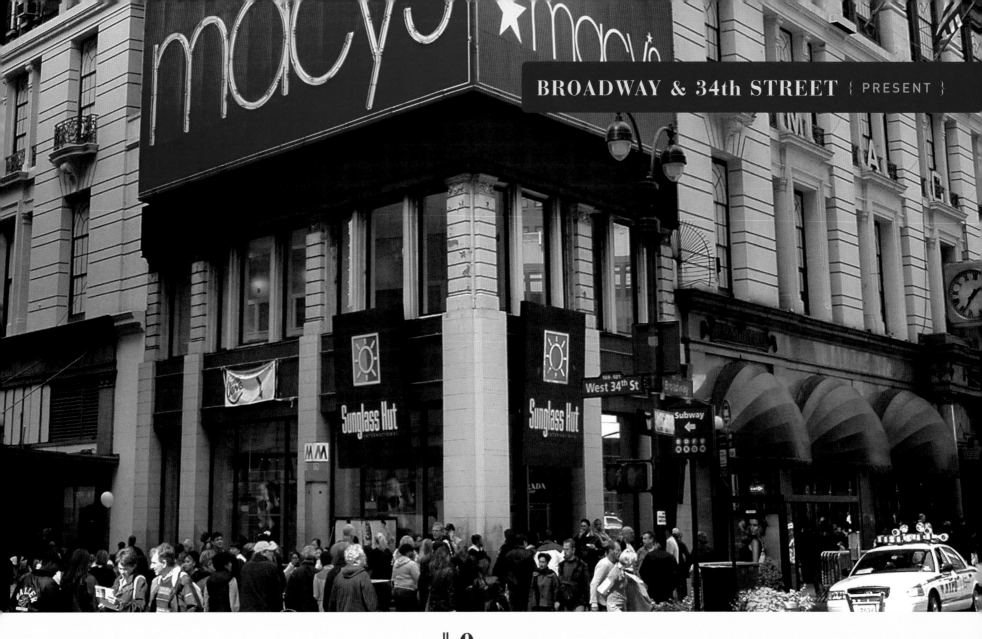

O ver the years, the notch brownstone building has seen its share of tenants come and go—from jewelers to liquor stores to restaurants to the Sunglass Hut that stands today. In the mid-1940s, Macy's—which claims to be "the world's largest store"—began advertising on the holdout's upper floors, which it rents annually. The original wooden escalators are still in operation at Macy's, which now boasts more than 800 additional locations across the nation.

PENNSYLVANIA STATION { PAST }

One of the architectural jewels of the city at the time, Pennsylvania Station—designed by Charles McKim of McKim, Mead & White and unveiled in 1910—was a masterpiece of pink-granite in the Beaux Arts style. Travelers to New York aboard the Pennsylvania Railroad were treated to a monumental entrance to the city, greeted by steel-and-glass train sheds and a breathtaking concourse. Twenty-two stone eagles weighing two tons each adorned the facade, and a waiting area, modeled after Roman baths with a 150-foot vaulted ceiling, filled many a visitor with awe.

In 1963, Pennsylvania Station was demolished in what late New York Senator Daniel Patrick Moynihan called "the great act of vandalism in the history of the city." In its place, an office tower and the new Madison Square Garden were constructed above the railroad tracks, effectively eliminating anything resembling the station's grand past. But a return to the grandeur of Pennsylvania Station is underway, as New York's General Post Office, above, is being remodeled to restore some of the past glory that fell victim to the wrecking ball. The station will be named for Moynihan.

Before the New York Library was built, the area between 40th and 42nd Streets on Fifth Avenue was home to the Croton Reservoir, pictured here, which was built in 1842 to meet the demand for fresh water on the island of Manhattan. Water from the Croton River, forty miles north, was transported through underground pipes and an aqueduct in northern Manhattan. The aqueduct was later drained and filled to create the Great Lawn in Central Park, and the Croton Reservoir was demolished in 1899.

The New York Public Library today is one of the most beautiful buildings in New York. Designed by the architectural firm of Carrere and Hastings, the Beaux Arts building opened in 1911 after bequests from John Jacob Astor, Samuel J. Tilden, and Andrew Carnegie. The two famed lions guarding the Fifth Avenue entrance were designed by Edward Clark Potter and later nicknamed "Patience" and "Fortitude" by Mayor Fiorello LaGuardia in the 1930s. The Public Library's main building remains one of the leading research libraries in the world and contains a Gutenberg Bible from the year 1455; and the *Philosophiae Naturalis Principia Mathematica*, published by Sir Isaac Newton in 1687; and Thomas Jefferson's manuscript copy of the Declaration of Independence.

Collection of the New York Historical Society negative number 9206

Built between 1903 and 1913, Grand Central Terminal—seen here in a photograph from 1928—replaced an old terminal, which was torn down in phases in 1900. Designed by the architectural firms of Reed and Stern and Warren and Wermore, the new terminal featured architectural details of the Beaux Arts style. French sculptor Jules-Alexis Couton was hired to create what was the largest sculptural group in the world—a clock flanked by Mercury, Hercules, and Minerva that stood nearly 50 feet high facing south onto Park Avenue.

GRAND CENTRAL TERMINAL { PRESENT }

In 1996, Grand Central Terminal was restored to its 1913 splendor. The clock that looms over 42nd Street and Park Avenue contains the world's largest example of Tiffany glass, and at night the terminal is grandly lit and can be seen in the distance as far downtown as Union Square on 14th Street. The terminal has been a backdrop for many feature films over the years, including *North by Northwest*, *Men in Black*, and *Sky Captain and the World of Tomorrow*.

Collection of the New York Historical Society negative number 70587

Completed in 1913, Grand Central Terminal's interior features an information booth in the center of the concourse that has been a pre-arranged meeting place for countless New Yorkers over the years. The ceiling, painted in 1912 by French artist Paul Cesar Helleu, is unusual in that the sky is backward and the stars are slightly displaced. Some people believe this was an error on the part of the artist! Nine stories above the ground, a catwalk was built, making it possible to walk along the windows.

Damage from cigarette smoke obscured the ceiling for decades, turning the plaster a grimy black, but in 1999, the ceiling was restored to its original luster. A hub of fine restaurants graces the Main Concourse, including Cipriani, Dolci, and Charlie Palmer's Metrazur. The Oyster Bar & Restaurant, which opened in 1913, is still located on the lower level, and Grand Central Market is located on the east end of the terminal. Grand Central hosts numerous events, fairs, and showcases over the course of the year and on weekends.

Robert Moses: New York's Master Builder

"Those who can, build. Those who can't, criticize."

—ROBERT MOSES

He wasn't an architect. He wasn't a politician. He had no background in law, and he only learned planning while on the job. But Robert Moses had a vision for the country, and his laboratory was New York. And by the mid-20th century, he had became the most powerful person in New York City government and his work had influenced the design and planning of major cities from coast to coast.

Born in New Haven, Connecticut, on December 18, 1888, the son of a well-to-do department store owner, Moses went on to study at Yale, where he was a member of the swim team. It was a form of exercise Moses continued on a daily basis through out his life. During the Depression, he built more than a dozen gigantic public swimming pools in some of the 658 playgrounds he was responsible for planning.

In the early 1920s, Moses became known as a young reformer—part of Governor Al Smith's inner circle—and in 1926, he became chairman of the New York State Council of Parks. Over the next forty-two years, Moses built parks, highways, bridges, playgrounds, housing, civic centers, tunnels, and beaches, single-handedly controlling billions of dollars by eventually holding twelve appointed positions simultaneously, including Chairman of the Triborough Bridge Tunnel Authority and head of the State Power Commission. So powerful was Moses that at one point, one-fourth of federal construction dollars were being spent in the state of New York, and Moses had more than 80,000 workers under his command.

"We live in a motorized civilization."

—ROBERT MOSES

Robert Moses's vision for New York was imagined on a grand scale. He saw the city as a tower-filled metropolis, with more highways than any city on earth. It was this vision—built around the dream of automobiles and the thrill of the open road—that provided ammunition for many of Moses's harshest critics, who charged that the builder's preference for highways over public transportation was short-sighted and displaced thousands of people in New York. Some critics blamed Moses and his urban planning for the decay of the South Bronx and the uprooting of the Brooklyn Dodgers to Los Angeles. But there can be no denying that Robert Moses

ROBERT MOSES

Moses stands before a model of his proposed Brooklyn-Battery Bridge—a plan that was killed in 1939 by the Roosevelt Administration. The Brooklyn-Battery Tunnel was built instead.

THROGS NECK BRIDGE

Moses oversaw the planning and construction of the Throgs Neck Bridge, which links the Bronx and Queens and opened in 1961.

TRIBOROUGH BRIDGE

This aerial view shows the three spans of the Triborough Bridge, which opened in 1936. Connecting Manhattan, Queens, and the Bronx, the bridge carries more than 200,000 vehicles per day today.

VERRAZANO-NARROWS BRIDGE

The Verrazano-Narrows Bridge was the world's longest suspension span when it opened in 1964. The Bridge connects Brooklyn with Staten Island and was named for Giovanni da Verrazano, who sailed into New York Harbor in 1524.

UNITED NATIONS HEADQUARTERS

Built in 1949 overlooking the East River on First Avenue between 41st and 42nd Streets, the UN officially opened on January 9, 1951.

FIORELLO H. LAGUARDIA

Mayor of New York for three terms from 1934 to 1945, "the Little Flower" as he was known (the Italian translation of his first name), worked closely with Robert Moses in many WPA (Works Projects Administration) projects.

greatly altered the landscape of New York City, warts and all.

Moses built housing for thousands of low- and middle-income New Yorkers—rows of red brick high-rise apartments with concrete playgrounds. His critics labeled them monotonous. He built golf courses, renovated the much-neglected Central Park Zoo, and oversaw the construction of highways to Long Island beaches, which he preserved as state land. Ironically, the man who considered the automobile essential to so many of his projects, never learned to drive one himself—instead maintaining a staff of limousine drivers which he kept on twenty-four–hour call.

The Triborough Bridge, completed in 1936, connected three boroughs—the Bronx, Queens, and Manhattan—and was an integral link in his vast network of parks and highways.

The project was finished two years after Moses ran for governor as a Republican against incumbent Herbert H. Lehman. In the campaign, Moses showed the public the aggressive, antagonistic style that had made him such an effective behind-the-scenes force in government. But voters did not like what they saw and overwhelmingly rejected the conservative Moses in the voting booths. Moses, however, was not discouraged. Instead, he was instrumental in bringing the United Nations to New York City.

In the late 1950s, the city was plagued with urban renewal scandals. Moses bore the brunt of them, when some of his associates were implicated in bilking slum tenants with high rents. His power began to decline, and his appointment as president of the 1964–65 New York World's Fair seemed to some an opportunity for Moses to

reclaim a final moment of glory before retiring from public life.

In 1968, Moses lost control of the Triborough Bridge and Tunnel Authority and was made a consultant, thus officially ending his reign as New York's power broker. Because Robert Moses, in the majority of his projects, resorted to the destruction of existing buildings and the displacement of residents, many critics of urban planning have not been kind to the master builder in recent years.

Moses was criticized for showing a bias toward big business and the upper classes, and often seemed to design with their best interests in mind. But considering Moses accomplished the majority of his sprawling, ambitious projects during the Great Depression, his contributions to the conservation and preservation of parks, open spaces, and roadways is remarkable.

Collection of the New York Historical Society negative number 58798

Chelsea Piers opened in 1910 to much fanfare. Even before the docks were officially opened, the world's most famous luxury liners, such as the *Lusitania* and *Mauretania*, were docking there. The "unsinkable" *Titanic* was scheduled to arrive on April 16, 1912, though fate intervened two days earlier. By the 1930s, however, transatlantic travel by ship dropped considerably, halting almost completely by the 1950s, when commercial airlines became more popular. The last big tenants relocated to New Jersey in 1967, bringing an end to the shipping business at Chelsea Piers.

Beginning in 1995, the Chelsea Piers Sports and Entertainment Complex, situated on Piers 59–62, opened in stages. A field house, golf complex, skating rink, bowling alleys, restaurants, and spa revitalized the long-neglected waterfront property. Silver Screen Studios has 200,000 square feet of production space, where television shows, feature films, and fashion shoots are produced, and Chelsea Piers has become a popular destination for outings, birthday parties, and recreation-seeking New Yorkers. The piers also dock touring and wedding yachts, which travel the waters around Manhattan for parties and events.

WAKE UP YOUR ENERGY!

GEORGIA COLEMAN
OLYMPIC DIVING CHAMPION

COSTLIER TOBACCOS

HYGRADE FRANKFURTERS

LOANS

RIVAL BEAUTY PARLORS

CRAWFORD CLOTHES

BILLIARDS

NEW AMSTERDAM

DANCING 150 DANCE PARTNERS

The major crosstown thoroughfare in Manhattan, 42nd Street has been part of New York and the world's lingo since the beginning of the 20th century. The stretch of theaters between 7th and 8th Avenues—thanks to Oscar Hammerstein, "the Father of Times Square"—became the most celebrated entertainment district the world had ever seen. Along 42nd Street, theaters such as the Lyric, the Harris, the New Amsterdam, the Selwyn, and the Empire dotted the landscape until the area was completely redesigned in the 1990s. The McGraw-Hill Building, an Art Deco structure built in 1931, the same year as the Empire State Building, can be seen in the distance.

THE POWER TO WATCH
LIVE TV ON YOUR PHONE.

By the late 1990s, 42nd Street began to undergo a renaissance. The city government encouraged a clean-up of Times Square, as the area had, by the 1960s, become home to a number of porn houses and sex-related shops along the strip between 7th and 8th Avenues, creating an entire subculture. Today, 42nd Street is home to numerous national chain stores, theaters, museums, and restaurants looking to maximize exposure along the famous, flashing strip visited by thousands of tourists every day. Nearly all of the buildings and theaters on this block have been torn down and replaced, but the McGraw-Hill Building, between 8th and 9th Avenues, remains.

Times Square is a small but bright patch of concrete at the intersection of Broadway and Seventh Avenue between 42nd and 47th Streets. Though composed of just a few city blocks, it's one of the most photographed places on earth. The square was named after the headquarters of the *New York Times,* which used to be located in a tower on 42nd Street. In 1904, New York Mayor George B. McClellan renamed the area Times Square, and in 1907, the first ball was dropped from the Times Building tower, signifying the New Year.

The *New York Times* is nearby, but the newspaper no longer has offices in the tower it occupied until 1913. Today, many of the neon signs have given way to giant television-style signs that pump commercial advertising onto the streets. In fact, Times Square is the only neighborhood that includes a mandatory zoning ordinance that requires tenants to display brightly lit signs. Some of the businesses in the Times Square area include the ABC television network, Virgin Records, Morgan Stanley, Viacom, Condé Nast Publications, and Reuters.

CHEVROLET

Pepsodent
On the Air with
TOOTH PASTE
Removes film from Teeth

The area around Duffy Square has long been a hub of theaters, music, hotels, and restaurants, as well as an area for both business and celebration. New Year's Eve revelers have been gathering around the square since 1907 to watch the famous Waterford crystal ball drop a few blocks downtown at Times Square. Duffy Square sits right in the middle of some of the world's greatest advertising campaigns, as seen here in this photograph of the busy intersection from the 1930s.

DUFFY SQUARE { PRESENT }

LORE & LEGEND

Times Square has had its share of street performers gather at Duffy Square over the years, and the Naked Cowboy, pictured here, is the latest star.

A statue commemorating George M. Cohan (1878–1942) stands at Duffy Square on the southern end of the triangle at 46th Street where Broadway meets 7th Avenue. The inscription quotes his most famous song, "Give My Regards to Broadway." Here, Cohan's statue is boxed in plywood for protection while a brand new TKTS pavilion (where tickets to Broadway shows can be bought) is built. To the north of Cohan's statue stands another statue unveiled in 1937 and dedicated to Father Francis Patrick Duffy, a military chaplain during World War I.

CITY IN TIME | NEW YORK 103

The midtown blocks of Fifth Avenue were mostly a residential district for New York's social elite at the turn of the 20th century. Edith Wharton, in her Pulitzer Prize–winning novel *The Age of Innocence* (1920), describes the lives of the aristocratic families who lived along this famous thoroughfare in the 1870s. Construction on St. Patrick's Cathedral at 50th Street and Fifth Avenue commenced in 1858, and after being halted during the Civil War, was finally completed in 1878. It is the largest decorated Gothic-style Catholic cathedral in North America.

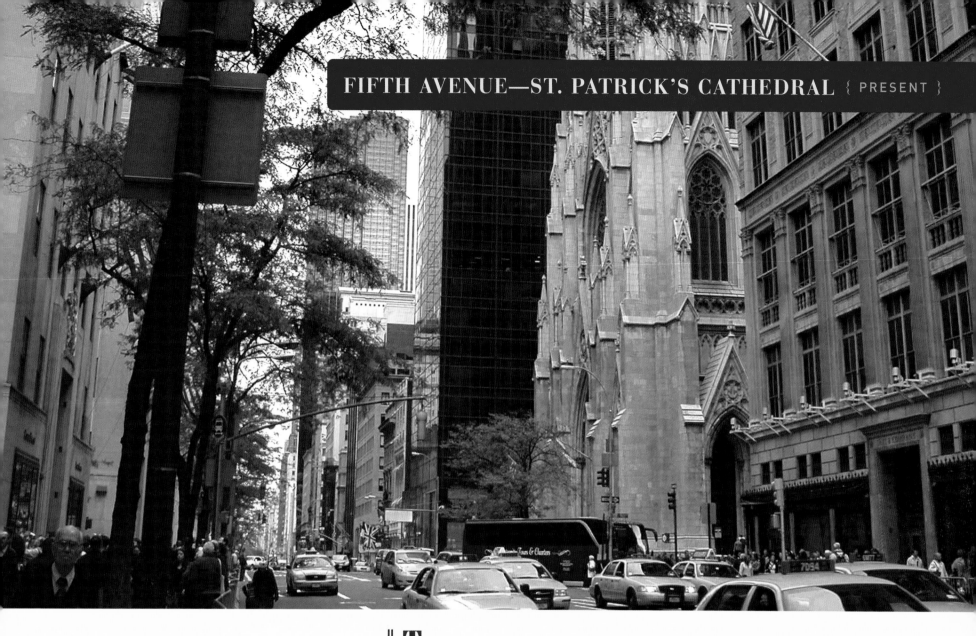

Today, the midtown blocks of Fifth Avenue are famously commercial and deserving of the moniker, "most expensive street in the world." In 1924, Horace Saks and Bernard Gimbel opened Saks Fifth Avenue, the upscale department store, in the building just across 49th Street from St. Patrick's Cathedral. On the west side of Fifth Avenue, directly across from the famous church and department store, is Rockefeller Plaza—a complex of nineteen commercial buildings, many in the Art Deco style built in the 1930s, and now home to General Electric and Radio City Music Hall.

Just above the most famous stretch of Broadway were the offices of most of the entertainment industry and theaters—such as Warners, seen here—that showed the popular silent films of the time, such as Syd Chaplin's *The Missing Link* and John Barrymore's *When a Man Loves*. This section of Broadway north of Times Square had many residents who lived along this famous stretch of New York City.

Theaters, hotels, and restaurants continue to line Broadway at the stretch between 51st and 54th Streets, but the street is mainly comprised of offices and stores, as residents have mostly been driven out. The CBS program *Late Show with David Letterman* inhabits the Ed Sullivan Theater, while the Broadway Theater is currently running *Oprah Winfrey Presents: The Color Purple*, based on Alice Walker's Pulitzer Prize–winning novel. The Broadway Theatre opened as B.S. Moss's Colony Theatre on December 25, 1924, and was originally a silent film house.

THE PLAZA HOTEL { PAST }

The Plaza Hotel is a nineteen-story landmark building on the corner of Fifth Avenue and Central Park South. The French Renaissance chateau-style hotel was designed by Henry Janeway Hardenbergh and officially opened on October 1, 1907. Celebrities such as Mark Twain, Groucho Marx, and F. Scott Fitzgerald were among its guests in its early years, and no doubt found time to frequent the hotel's windowless Oak Bar. The hotel's Persian Room and Palm Court were also popular gathering places for the famous and well-heeled.

LORE & LEGEND

The Plaza Hotel has had many famous residents and guests over the years, but perhaps none so famous as author Kay Thompson's Eloise. The main character in Thompson's *Eloise*, written in 1956, is a precocious and ebullient six-

year-old girl who lives in the room on the "tippy-top floor with her little dog, Weenie and her turtle Skipperdee." Thompson has said that she based Eloise on her goddaughter, Liza Minnelli.

Donald Trump purchased the hotel in 1988 but lost money when he sold it to a member of the Saudi Royal family seven years later. In 2004, Elad Properties purchased The Plaza Hotel for $675 million and closed it in the spring of 2005 for renovations that will result in 282 hotel rooms and 152 upscale condominiums. The Plaza's main entrance faces Grand Army Plaza and the Pulitzer Fountain, where the Roman goddess of fruits and nuts, Pomona, is portrayed.

SHERMAN MONUMENT { PAST }

Designed by sculptor Augustus Saint-Gaudens, the gilded bronze equestrian statue of Civil War general William Tecumseh Sherman was placed at Central Park's main entrance in 1903. But when the Pulitzer Fountain was designed for the southern half of Grand Army Plaza in 1913, the Sherman Monument was moved, for reasons of symmetry, to the southeast entrance, across the street from the Plaza Hotel. Sherman spent the last years of his life in New York City, where he was devoted to the theater, enjoyed painting, and made the rounds as a colorful and much-in-demand speaker. He died in February 1891.

A year after Sherman's death, this monument was commissioned by members of the City's Chamber of Commerce—many of whom were good friends of the general. The allegorical figure of peace walking before Sherman was modeled after Saint-Gaudens' mistress, Davida Johnson, and the pine branch at the horse's feet was designed to represent the general's march though Georgia during the Civil War.

Bordered by Columbus Circle to the west and Fifth Avenue to the east, Central Park South (59th Street) is home to some of the most famous hotels in New York. The Plaza, the Ritz-Carlton, and the Essex House were not yet built in 1889 when this photograph was taken, but the Central Park Hotel was a sign of things to come for this prestigious block in midtown Manhattan.

Central Park South today is home not only to the Plaza, Ritz-Carlton, and the Jumeirah Essex House as it's now known, but also to Mickey Mantle's restaurant, the New York Athletic Club, and many upscale condominiums, including the Trump Parc apartments, the Coronet Apartments, and the St. Moritz Apartment Hotel. Central Park South still has horse-drawn carriages running up and down its length, taking tourists in and out of the park, day and night.

Central Park

City commissioners recognized the need for a substantial park and sponsored a competition in 1857 to select a plan. But the idea met with some resistance. An editor for the *Journal of Commerce* wrote, "There is no need of turning one-half of the island into a permanent forest for the accommodation of loafers. The grand park scheme is humbug and

By the middle of the 19th century, there were more than half a million people cluttered in tenement houses in lower Manhattan, and space was dwindling. Ports and shipyards were taking over the shorelines, so access to the water was virtually eliminated. The noise level was growing and open spaces were disappearing at an alarming rate.

William Cullen Bryant, editor of the *Evening Post*, was among the first to call for a large public park to augment the relatively small squares of parkland and cemeteries dotting the downtown landscape where many New York City residents were finding refuge.

the sooner it is abandoned the better."

A total of 33 anonymous entries were presented, and the commissioners eventually chose the "Greensward Plan" by Frederick Law Olmsted and Calvert Vaux. Olmsted was inspired by the vast public parks he saw while in Europe, and he and Vaux set out to create what would ultimately

become an oasis of serenity in the middle of Manhattan. But in 1858, when construction of Central Park began in earnest, the acreage was by no means "central" to anything. It was a vast, rocky wilderness, far north of New York's population, and the majority of the thousands who built it had to travel an hour north of the Lower East Side where they lived.

Olmsted and Vaux began by blasting large sections of the earth, since terrain was rocky and there was little soil to accommodate the trees and shrubs they wanted to plant in the park. Gigantic explosions echoed around the city on a daily basis as the terrain was prepared for the ambitious design. Italian stonecutters mixed

with Irish and German laborers, with pay at just a dollar a day. The work was dangerous, and injuries on the job often were fatal. A draining system ultimately was installed below ground where some four million trees representing more than a thousand species were planted. Thirty-six bridges were built, and four man-made bodies of water were constructed. Roadways were built leading to the Mall, and at its center was Bethesda Terrace—the place Olmsted and Vaux envisioned as the "grand promenade."

Covering some 843 acres, the Greensward Plan called for a series of stunning vistas and serene views at nearly every turn. A sheep meadow, pastoral ponds with willow trees looming, winding paths and streams, stone bridges, and even a castle would dot the landscape.

Olmsted and Vaux had the foresight to envision a day when their park would indeed become "Central Park," surrounded by the grid system that the city fathers had planned long ago. "The time will come," Olmsted predicted, "when New York will be built up, when all the grading and filling will be done, and when the picturesquely varied, rocky formations of the Island will have been converted into rows of monotonous straight streets and piles of erect buildings."

In 1878—twenty years after the first shovels were first laid to the area now known as Central Park—the Greensward Plan was complete. Despite resigning many times, Olmsted and Vaux managed to live to see the fruits of their labor, weathering the likes of Boss Tweed and the Civil War.

By the end of the 19th century, demand for the very space Olmsted and Vaux had envisioned threatened to ruin Central Park. Money for park maintenance and improvements began to run dry, and before long, trees were dying and litter and vandalism were on the rise. It wasn't until the election of Fiorello LaGuardia in 1934 that Central Park restoration was given serious attention. The 1960s, however, marked another turn for the worse, as the park had begun to deteriorate again. Graffiti, vandalism, and lawlessness prevailed throughout the park well into the 1970s.

An improving economy in the 1980s enabled the Conservancy to raise millions for restoration projects, and today, Central Park is once again the oasis of serenity that Olmsted and Vaux envisioned nearly 150 years ago.

CENTRAL PARK FACTS

- Central Park is completely man-made and cost roughly $200 million (in today's dollars) to build.

- There are 51 sculptures in the Park.

- There are nearly 6,000 benches that, placed end-to-end, would extend for 7 miles.

- Central Park has 21 playgrounds.

- More than 25 million people visit Central Park each year.

This photograph from 1888 shows horse-drawn coaches and single riders parading through scenic Central Park on a Sunday—a weekend event made popular by New York's wealthy in the late 19th century. Groups such as The New York Coaching Club—formed in 1875 by Colonel Delancey Astor Kane and Willie Jay—helped elevate the sport of driving to an art. Also popular at the time were high-wheel bicycles, which both men and women of the 19th century enjoyed.

CENTRAL PARK COACHINGS { PRESENT }

G one are the high-wheel bicycles, but horse-drawn carriages still roam through Central Park, carrying tourists rather than New York's social elite. Pedicabs have become popular in recent years, as tourists and even working New Yorkers in a hurry flag down these bicycle carriages to take a ride through the park. Bicyclists, rollerbladers, joggers, and kids on scooters join the carriages on the roads of Central Park for exercise or sightseeing.

When Frederick Law Olmsted and Calvert Vaux unveiled plans for Central Park in 1858, they proposed an architectural "heart of the Park" that would be defined by a sweeping promenade overlooking the Lake. This image was taken in September 1862, when the terrace was still under construction. This is the only structure in Central Park designed by Olmsted and Vaux that was not meant to peacefully blend in with the natural settings of the park.

M ore than 140 years after it was built, the Bethesda Terrace, with its decorative elements by English-born architect Jacob Wrey Mould, still remains the heart of Central Park. Here undergoing cleaning and repair, the Terrace is a popular gathering place for exercising mothers, wedding portraits, and picnics. As Olmsted and Vaux intended, Bethesda Terrace is still the centerpiece of Central Park, and the growth of the trees around it have made the Terrace even more spectacular as one approaches from the Mall just south of it.

CENTRAL PARK—GAPSTOW BRIDGE { PAST }

The original Gapstow Bridge was designed by Jacob Wrey Mould and constructed in 1874, but its wooden design with cast-iron railings did not last more than twenty years. The bridge was rebuilt with sturdy stone, in a design that compliments the water and woodlands area around it, and is one of the first of many serene yet quietly spectacular views that visitors to the park encounter upon entering Central Park through the Grand Army Plaza at 59th Street and Fifth Avenue on the southeast corner of the park.

Today, the ivy that covers most of the Gapstow Bridge only serves to blend the stone bridge into the pastoral setting of the park. Grand Army Plaza is the most popular entrance to Central Park, and the view of the skyline looking South from the bridge underscores the beauty of the park oasis that sits in the very center of New York City. Frederick Law Olmsted and Calvert Vaux expected the Grand Army Plaza entrance to be the most used entrance in Central Park, and they wanted this initial walk-in to be among the most pleasing views the park offered.

Located at the intersection of Broadway, Central Park West, Central Park South, and 8th Avenue, Columbus Circle marks the southwest corner of Central Park and was completed in 1905. The monument in the center of the traffic circle was erected in 1892 to commemorate the 400th anniversary of the Italian voyager's first trip to the Americas. The monument consists of a marble statue of Columbus, with bronze reliefs representing the *Niña*, the *Pinta*, and the *Santa Maria*.

Today, Columbus Circle is flanked by the Trump International Hotel and Tower to the north, and the Time Warner Center, the Shops at Columbus Circle, and Jazz at Lincoln Center to the west. In 1913, the Maine Monument was erected to honor sailors killed aboard the battleship *USS Maine* in 1898. This monument is located on the northeast side of the circle, at the Merchants' Gate entrance to Central Park.

Collection of the New York Historical Society, negative number 55734

Central Park West forms the western edge of Central Park and is the eastern-most Avenue on the Upper West Side. Central Park West runs 51 blocks from Columbus Circle at 59th Street to Frederick Douglass Circle at 110th Street. The Second Church of Christ Scientist on the west side of the street was designed by Frederick R. Comstock and completed in 1901. The church is notable for a green dome that sits atop its neo-Classical base.

Central Park West is home to many magnificent buildings, including The San Remo, the El Dorado, The Beresford, The Majestic, and The Dakota. Most were built during the 1930s, replacing the 19th-century hotels that bore the same names. The American Museum of Natural History and Rose Center for Earth and Space are located on Central Park West, and the building at 55 Central Park West was made famous as "Spook Central" in the 1984 blockbuster movie *Ghostbusters*.

Designed by architect Henry Janeway Hardenbergh, The Dakota is located on the northwest corner of Central Park West and 72nd Street. It was completed in 1884 and is believed to have been given its name because, at the time, the area was so remote that it was considered comparable to the Dakota Territory. Built around an inner courtyard, The Dakota originally had sixty-five apartments—none of which were alike—and stood nine stories high. At the time, the Dakota towered above the landscape of the area now known as the Upper West Side.

LORE & LEGEND

Director Roman Polanski photographed The Dakota's exteriors for his 1967 movie, *Rosemary's Baby*. the popular horror film. The Dakota is also featured in Jack Finney's novel, *Time and Again*.

Since its inception, The Dakota has been a popular building for New York's high society to call their home—or perhaps their second home. And the same is true today. The building is best known as the site where former Beatle John Lennon was murdered on the night of December 8, 1980, as he was returning home to his apartment there. His widow, Yoko Ono, still lives in the building, as does their son, Sean Lennon. Other famous residents have included Lauren Bacall, Judy Garland, Paul Simon, Gilda Radner, Bono, and Sting.

Founded in 1869 by Theodore Roosevelt Sr., the father of President Theodore Roosevelt, the American Museum of Natural History had its first home in the old Arsenal building in Central Park until the H. H. Richardson Beaux Arts design was completed on Central Park West in 1936. Designed by John Russell Pope, the Roman entrance on Central Park West stands as a monument to Teddy Roosevelt and leads to a Roman basilica, which has long been home to the skeleton of a barosaurus defending her young from an allosaurus.

LORE & LEGEND

The museum held the largest sapphire in the world, The Star of India, until it was stolen, along with several other precious stones, on October 29, 1964. Jack Murphy, a former surfing champion, and his accomplices climbed

through a bathroom window they had unlocked earlier in the day. The Star of India was later recovered in a locker at a bus depot in Miami, but another stone, the Eagle Diamond, presumably was recut and never recovered.

Today, the famous, full-size model of a Blue Whale is suspended in the Milstein Family Hall of Ocean Life. Children and adults alike are drawn to the museum for its constantly changing dinosaur exhibits, but permanent collections such as the life-size dioramas of human predecessors still attract visitors in droves. In February 2000, the adjoining Hayden Planetarium was redesigned and became part of the Rose Center for Earth and Space, which features a seven-story glass cube designed by James Polshek.

One of the largest and most important art museums in the world, The Metropolitan Museum of Art, known to most as "The Met," was founded after a group of prominent American art lovers in the Union League returned from Paris in 1866 and demanded America have its own national institution for art. The museum had several smaller buildings until collections grew and more space was needed to display the impressive art that was being acquired. The building in its permanent space on Fifth Avenue at 81st Street was designed by Calvert Vaux, one of the architects of Central Park, and Jacob Wrey Mould and opened in 1880. The Beaux Arts facade was designed by Richard Morris Hunt and completed in 1926.

Americans in Paris
1860–1900

Over the years, several additions and floors have been added to the Met, expanding the original structure considerably. The museum now measures almost a quarter mile along the "Museum Mile" section of Fifth Avenue and occupies more than two million square feet—twenty times the size of the original building. The museum's permanent collection contains more than two million works of art from around the world, including extensive Egyptian, Asian, and African art, as well as paintings and sculptures by nearly all the European masters.

Located in Riverside Park at 122nd Street, Grant's Tomb is a mausoleum containing the bodies of Ulysses S. Grant and his wife, Julia Dent Grant. Grant was the American General for the Union in the Civil War and became President of the United States in 1869. John Duncan designed this marble and granite structure (officially known as General Grant National Memorial), which was dedicated on April 27, 1897—twelve years after Grant's death and with nearly one million people in attendance.

Time was not kind to Grant's Tomb, as the monument fell into a severe state of disrepair by the 1960s. Defaced with graffiti, the majestic structure became a hangout for late-night revelers, and the public grew tired of what had become an eyesore. However, as sentimental interest in the Civil War grew toward the end of the 20th century, Grant's relatives threatened to remove the remains and have them buried somewhere else. In the mid-1990s the National Park Service pledged nearly $2 million to restore the memorial to its present condition.

After the turn of the 20th century, the area just north of Central Park became infused with blacks from the West Indies and the southern United States. The thoroughfare of 125th Street has long been considered the "Main Street of Harlem" and cuts from east to west across Manhattan. The Apollo Theater rose to prominence during the Harlem Renaissance in the years before World War II and was the cornerstone of nightlife along 125th Street, launching the numerous careers of some of America's most famous entertainers, such as Ella Fitzgerald.

LORE & LEGEND

Blumstein's department store—whose sign is still displayed prominently at 230 West 125th Street even though the store has been gone for decades—was the site of some of Harlem's most historic moments. The Blumstein family built

the $1 million store in 1923, and though mostly blacks shopped there, Blumstein's employed very few beyond menial positions and elevator operators. In 1934, a successful boycott resulted in the hiring of thirty-five black employees.

Economic forces plunged Harlem into "ghettofication" during World War II— buildings fell into such disrepair that they were abandoned, empty shells. For decades, Harlem was overridden with crime, drugs, and poverty. But in the late 1990s, gentrification and a booming economy made funding for new developments more accessible, and many of Harlem's beautiful brownstones were restored to their glorious conditions. The neighborhood has enjoyed a startling commercial and residential rebirth, but some worry that the price may be the loss of black culture.

I n 1892, the Harlem Speedway—a $5 million roadway project—was built along the Harlem River at 155th Street extending to Dyckman Street so that the rich could trot their horses and the not-so-rich could watch the "sulkies" (one-manned, two-wheeled carriages pulled by the horse) pass by. The horses did attract spectators who gathered on the rock bluffs above. But the advent of the automobile eventually saw to it that the speedway was used less and less, and resentment against public funding for the playground for the privileged began to build.

By 1918, it was estimated that fewer than 20 horse-drawn carriages a day were making use of the Speedway, and the following year, the road was opened to automobiles. The Harlem River Drive, as envisioned by Robert Moses, was built and completed in 1964, extending the Speedway from the Triborough Bridge to north of the George Washington Bridge. In 2003, the parkway was re-designated the "369th Harlem Hellfighters Drive" in recognition of the all-black regiment that served in World War I.

The skyline in downtown Manhattan was forever changed on September 11, 2001, when the Twin Towers fell. While many New Yorkers confess to never having appreciated the Towers' design, they just as easily admit to missing their vast presence in the skyline. Rebuilding the downtown skyline, many politicians believed, was a priority, and a necessary symbol of America's resolve. After years of political wrangling and design changes, construction on the new World Trade Center complex began in 2006.

One World Trade Center, or Freedom Tower, is set to be completed in 2011 or 2012, and will become the tallest building in the United States, surpassing Chicago's Sears Tower. The Freedom Tower's spire will stand 1,776 feet high as a tribute to the year the Declaration of Independence was drafted. Freedom Tower will have 2.6 million square feet of office space on 124 floors, as well as an observation deck at 1,362 feet. Several new accompanying skyscrapers will complete the future World Trade Center complex, which promises to make the New York skyline whole again.

New York City at Night

TIMES SQUARE
was always "the great white way" of New York at night.
This is the Times Building in 1908.

New York is known as "the city that never sleeps." New Yorkers do, in fact, sleep. It's just that there are seemingly millions more who are nocturnal creatures—who flow into the city from the outer boroughs, New Jersey, Westchester, and Long Island for the nightlife that only Manhattan offers. Or they have night jobs and do the reverse commute, venturing into the city against the traffic as the masses are just heading home for dinner.

At night, the hotels are still heavily staffed, the bars are packed, and the taxis form an endless yellow stream down Fifth Avenue and up Madison. The theater district around Times Square bustles as folks leaving restaurants try to catch a Broadway show on time. People flow up the escalators at Penn Station straight upstairs to Madison Square Garden for a Knicks or Rangers game. Men decked out in tuxedos and women in sequined gowns head to Lincoln Center for the opera. Street performers abound, like the street musician playing the sax—with his hat set out for tips—providing the theme music to a New York night.

Below ground, the daily commuters are gone, and the crowds in subway cars thin out some, but there are still places to go, and any New Yorker will tell you the subway beats anything else for getting around quickly.

THE GUGGENHEIM MUSEUM
on Fifth Avenue and 89th Street. Architect Frank
Lloyd Wright died before its completion in 1959.

Downtown, in the West Village, cars thump along on cobblestone streets. Jazz clubs, tightly packed restaurants and cafes, and even late-night coffee shops are in full swing.

The Flatiron District, with its loft-like restaurants and shopping, takes on a whole new feel at night. The backpack crowd with their laptops and iPods move on, and the moneyed guys and gals from the financial world replace them, hopping out of town cars for late dinners along Park Avenue South.

Chinatown barely misses a beat, with the sidewalks just as packed as at midday, and the seafood markets along Canal and Mott Streets remain loud and busy. The East Village comes alive after dark at Astor Place and St. Mark's—with its tattoo parlors, vegetarian restaurants, and rock clubs gearing up for business once the sun goes down.

Down on Wall Street, things quiet down some. The crowds are gone, save for the young ones pulling long hours in pursuit of the big payday. After all, like the song says, if they can make it here, they can make it anywhere.

Most of the stores and lunch cafes are closed, as town cars gather to wait for those straggling late-night traders and dealmakers to finish their business. Once they climb in the back of the car, they're driven home to their apartments uptown, passing museums and libraries that hearken back to another time, when architects thought in stone rather than glass.

Central Park after dark has quieted down, as cars and taxis cross from the East to the West Side, giving passengers a skyline glimpse of a white-hot city that borders this green oasis. Tourists in horse-drawn carriages point at the classic buildings within their view—hotels like the Plaza and the Essex House.

In Harlem, the music of yesteryear can still be heard on lively 125th Street. The Apollo, with its inviting sign lit up and down the busy cross street, recalls another era. All around the town, week-night or weekend, the city breathes after dark.

ATLAS STANDS at Rockefeller Center directly across from St. Patrick's Cathedral on Fifth Avenue.

THE METROPOLITAN MUSEUM OF ART was founded in 1870 and moved to its present site on Fifth Avenue ten years later. This facade and entrance was completed in 1926.

THE CLOCK IN FRONT OF THE SHERRY-NETHERLAND HOTEL on Fifth Avenue and 59th Street, as the Plaza Hotel looms in the distance.

Resources for Further Exploration

New York: An Illustrated History.
Burns, Ric and James Sanders, with Lisa Ades.
New York: Alfred A. Knopf, 1999.
The companion guide to the PBS television series.

Gotham: A History of New York City to 1898.
Burrows, Edwin G. and Mike Wallace.
New York: Oxford University Press, 2000.
A detailed narrative of New York's beginnings.

The Mythic City: Photographs of New York 1925–1940.
Gottscho, Samuel H.
New York: Princeton Architectural Press, 2005.
New York's architectural marvels photographed during
the height of the Depression.

**A Historical Atlas of New York City: A Visual Celebration of 400
Years of New York City's History.**
Homberger, Eric.
New York: Owl Books, 2005.
With maps, illustrations, and drawings depicting
New York's rich past.

The Encyclopedia of New York City.
Jackson, Kenneth T.
New Haven: Yale University Press, 1995.
People, places, events, and experiences in New York
in this illustrated volume.

New York City: A Short History.
Lankevich, George.
New York: New York University Press, 2002.
A chronological history of New York portrayed through
mayoral terms.

Lost New York.
Silver, Nathan.
New York: Houghton Mifflin, 2000.
Stunning photos celebrating the architecture of New York City.

Forgotten New York: Views of a Lost Metropolis.
Walsh, Kevin.
New York: Collins, 2006.
An essential walking tour guide of the New York that even
lifetime New Yorkers don't know about.

Photo Credits

Page 2	Library of Congress	Page 53	Gilbert King	Page 100	Library of Congress
Page 5	Lewis W. Hine, George Eastman House	Page 54	George Eastman House	Page 101	Gilbert King
Page 6–7	Library of Congress	Page 55	Gilbert King	Page 102	Collection of the New York Historical Society negative number 58360
Page 8	Gilbert King	Page 56	Library of Congress		
Page 10	Currier & Ives, 1876	Page 57	Gilbert King	Page 103	Gilbert King
Page 11	Image Courtesy NASA	Page 58	George Eastman House	Page 104	Collection of the New York Historical Society negative number 57623
Page 12	Collection of the New York Historical Society negative number 50593	Page 59	Gilbert King		
		Page 60	Collection of the New York Historical Society	Page 105	Gilbert King
Page 13	Gilbert King	Page 61	Gilbert King	Page 106	Collection of the New York Historical Society
Page 14	Library of Congress	Page 62	George Eastman House	Page 107	Gilbert King
Page 15	Gilbert King	Page 63	Gilbert King	Page 108	Library of Congress
Page 16	Collection of the New York Historical Society negative number 2528	Page 64	Collection of the New York Historical Society negative number 78324d	Page 109	Gilbert King
				Page 110	George Eastman House
Page 17	Gilbert King	Page 65	Gilbert King	Page 111	Gilbert King
Page 18	Collection of the New York Historical Society negative number 78321d	Page 66	Collection of the New York Historical Society negative number 69521	Page 112	Collection of the New York Historical Society negative number 48180-A
Page 19	Gilbert King	Page 67	Gilbert King	Page 113	Gilbert King
Page 20	Library of Congress	Page 68	Library of Congress	Page 114	All photos Library of Congress
Page 21	Gilbert King	Page 69	Gilbert King	Page 115	Gilbert King
Page 22	George Eastman House	Page 70	Collection of the New York Historical Society	Page 116	Collection of the New York Historical Society negative number 64345
Page 23	Gilbert King	Page 71	Gilbert King		
Page 24	Collection of the New York Historical Society negative number 59174	Page 72	Library of Congress	Page 117	Gilbert King
		Page 73	Gilbert King	Page 118	Victor Prevost, George Eastman House
Page 25	Gilbert King	Page 74	Library of Congress	Page 119	Gilbert King
Page 26–27	All photos Library of Congress except Chrysler Building: Gilbert King	Page 75	Gilbert King	Page 120	Library of Congress
		Page 76–77	All photos Library of Congress	Page 121	Gilbert King
Page 28	Library of Congress	Page 78	Library of Congress	Page 122	Library of Congress
Page 29	Gilbert King	Page 79	Gilbert King	Page 123	Gilbert King
Page 30	George Eastman House	Page 80	Lewis W. Hine, George Eastman House	Page 124	Collection of the New York Historical Society negative number 55734
Page 31	Gilbert King	Page 81	Gilbert King		
Page 32	George Eastman House	Page 82	Library of Congress	Page 125	Gilbert King
Page 33	Gilbert King	Page 83	Gilbert King	Page 126	Library of Congress
Page 34	George Eastman House	Page 84	Collection of the New York Historical Society negative number 69523	Page 127	Gilbert King
Page 35	Gilbert King			Page 128	Library of Congress
Page 36	Library of Congress	Page 85	Gilbert King	Page 129	Gilbert King
Page 37	Gilbert King	Page 86	Library of Congress	Page 130	Library of Congress
Page 38	Library of Congress	Page 87	Gilbert King	Page 131	Gilbert King
Page 39	Gilbert King	Page 88	Library of Congress	Page 132	Library of Congress
Page 40	Collection of the New York Historical Society	Page 89	Gilbert King	Page 133	Gilbert King
Page 41	Gilbert King	Page 90	Collection of the New York Historical Society negative number 9206	Page 134	Morris Engel, George Eastman House
Page 42	Library of Congress			Page 135	Gilbert King
Page 43	Gilbert King	Page 91	Gilbert King	Page 136	Collection of the New York Historical Society
Page 44	Library of Congress	Page 92	Collection of the New York Historical Society negative number 70587	Page 137	Gilbert King
Page 45	Gilbert King			Page 138	Gilbert King
Page 46	Library of Congress	Page 93	Gilbert King	Page 139	Skidmore, Owings and Merrill
Page 47	Gilbert King	Page 94–95	All photos Library of Congress	Page 140–141	All photos Gilbert King
Page 48	Collection of the New York Historical Society	Page 96	Collection of the New York Historical Society negative number 58798		
Page 49	Gilbert King				
Page 50	All photos Library of Congress	Page 97	Gilbert King		
Page 51	Gilbert King	Page 98	Collection of the New York Historical Society		
Page 52	Library of Congress	Page 99	Gilbert King		

Index